DUNNOTTAR IN SCOTTISH HISTORY

Even if there were no castle at Dunnottar, the site would immediately catch the eye – an enormous flat-topped rock with sheer cliffs on three sides jutting out into the North Sea and attached to the mainland only by a narrow neck of land. But Dunnottar is more than a topographical curiosity: this rock and the buildings on it have reflected in miniature much of the rich and tragic story of Scottish history. St Ninian, William Wallace, Mary Queen of Scots and the Marquis of Montrose have all appeared on this dramatic stage. Most famously, though, it was at Dunnottar Castle that a small garrison held out against the might of Cromwell's army for eight months and saved the Scottish Crown Jewels, the 'Honours of Scotland', from destruction. The buildings bring history alive and vice versa.

Dun is a Pictish word meaning place of strength and the word Dunnottar, originally 'Dun Fother' probably means 'fort in the low country'. This seems a prosaic description for a dramatic place, but no more plausible translation has yet emerged. The castle lies in the 'Mearns', a name given to the land which is east of the Grampian Highlands between Montrose and Stonehaven. Long before North Sea oil, this area was prosperous; it has rich farmland and easy access to trading routes and fishing grounds.

It is also strategically important. For centuries the Mearns has provided the main access from central Scotland to the fertile Moray Firth plain and the Highlands beyond; and it just so happens that the narrowest gap between the Grampian mountains and the sea is opposite to Dunnottar Castle, from which this gateway can easily be patrolled. Thus a combination of wealth and strategic significance, combined with the perfect defensive site for a strongpoint, have thrust Dunnottar and its lands into the limelight of Scottish history.

GEOLOGY, BIRD AND ANIMAL LIFE

GEOLOGY

The rock of Dunnottar is as remarkable at close quarters as it is from a distance. Coming up the path to the castle, you see the curious effect created by red rock packed full with a variety of large pebbles and rocks like raisins in a fruitcake. Quite appropriately this conglomerate is known as 'pudding stone'; it results from erosion of the Grampian Highlands in a very arid climate about 400 million years ago.

The distinctive peninsular of Dunnottar is on the 'downthrow' side of the Highland Boundary fault and the intensity of the fault movement has caused the original rock strata, normally about level, to be thrown on their ends to dramatic effect. Originally there was a sharp ridge attaching the rock to the mainland, but this has been cut through and the edge made perpendicular to deny all access from the mainland, so further increasing security. Note though, that the tunnel through the rock on the right of the path is entirely man-made (though why man decided to make it is not clear).

The conglomerate forms a rock of immense durability, the pebbles consisting mainly of hard and ancient Highland rocks, while the cementing matter is so tough that faults or cracks pass not between the pebbles and their binding material but straight through the pebbles themselves. In contrast, the red sandstone of the castle itself wastes rapidly when exposed to the atmosphere and there are many wonderful examples of what is termed "differential weathering", the stone being frequently fretted out into patterns like a honeycomb.

The rock of Dunnottar

BIRD AND ANIMAL LIFE

The cliffs at Dunnottar provide a secure nesting site for a variety of birds – lots of herring gulls, but also fulmars with stiff wings and a call like a crow, the tiny unmistakable puffin and the elegant kittiwake with its dipped-in-ink wings. Guillemots and razorbills are regular visitors from the nearby nesting colonies at Fowlsheugh, and peregrine falcons are sometimes seen, on the look out for unwary seabirds or the many feral pigeons which frequent cliffs and castle. Out at sea you may glimpse dolphins and seals as well as skuas, shag, cormorant and eider duck.

Fulmars at their nest

3

OUTER DEFENCES

Ownership of a tower house was a crucial status symbol for a powerful nobleman in late 14th-century Scotland. No wonder then that Sir William Keith, already Marischal of Scotland and hence one of the King's principal officers, decided to build one as a monument to his power.

The solid tower house or 'keep', together with the 9-metre-high curtain wall that blocks the natural approach to the rock, provided Keith not just with prestige but also with welcome security. Just as the tower house commands our attention from far off, so the sentry on the parapet could see all those approaching and, if necessary, word was passed down to the guards at the gate to close the great door and lower the portcullis. You may have noticed that the great door used to be even greater – it was reduced in the 17th century.

Entranceway and portcullis (see opposite)

The path to the main entrance is dominated by a knife-edge ridge which used to have a low wall round the edge. Then, as any attacker prepared a battering ram to stave in the great door, the warriors on the parapet would have an assortment of boulders, arrows and boiling liquids available to make the task more challenging. In the 14th century you would not, however, have had to cope with grape shot from the building on the right of the door; this was not built for another 200 years. It is known as Benholm's Lodging after a relative of the Keith family who visited the castle often and lodged in this building.

The castle's 14th-century great door is set in a 9-metre-high curtain wall

INNER DEFENCES

Those who were allowed in would pass the magazine on the left, whilst on the right are the guards' quarters, connected in turn to the basement of Benholm's Lodging and a dank prison cell at the far end.

Continuing up the entrance way, the 17th-century visitor may perhaps have been confronted with four cannons packed with grapeshot at very close range; behind these is a guardroom, hacked out of the rock. Any raiding party would have to clear all these rooms before proceeding, or be vulnerable to attacks from the rear.

Our attackers then had a steep walk up a narrow defile, doubtless with muskets firing at them from every side, and to achieve the plateau, they must pass through two vaulted tunnels or 'pends', with bolted doors ahead of them and cannons above. And even if some did make it through the pends, they still had the keep to take!

From the second pend you emerge on to the remarkable grassy plateau. Move a few steps into the open space, from where you can see on the hill in the distance a memorial to the people of the district of Stonehaven who fell in two World Wars. Across the cut grass of the old bowling green, edged by the green banks of the 17th- century gun batteries, is a range of the Quadrangle. To your right is a ruined lodging house and behind and to your right is the Keep, the oldest part of the fortifications, where we suggest that you start your tour.

The bowling green

The Stonehaven War Memorial seen from the castle

The vaulted tunnels or 'pends'

THE KEEP

The 14th-century Keep is a sophisticated example of the Scottish tower house of the period. Bleak from the outside, it nevertheless contains all the 'mod-cons' of the late 14th century.

Just above the door is an arched niche for the effigy of a patron saint; this relic of medieval piety was quite common in Scottish castles. The Keep was originally defended by a stout wooden door – you can see the fixings for its hinges and bolts in the sides of the opening. The door opens into a small lobby with an alcove on the right where the porter would have kept the keys and a lamp to light the foot of the staircase to the first floor. The steps straight ahead lead down to the vaulted basement under the main block of the tower. This was originally a cellar but was later converted into a spacious kitchen. You can see the huge fireplace on the left with stone seats on either side; the small window at the far end held a sink. In the corner to your left a doorway leads through into a smaller cellar in the wing with a tiny prison cell built under the staircase opening from it. Both vaulted cellars originally had timber-floored lofts – you can see the projecting stones which once supported the floor beams.

The straight steps to the upper floor originally had a door at their foot. The first opening from them is the partly blocked entrance to the castle's original kitchen in the wing. This was converted into a private room when the kitchen was moved down to the cellars, but you can still see the old fireplace in the end wall (and if you crawl in you can also see the old oven!).

The great hall, a few steps up, was the heart of life in a medieval castle. It was not simply a feasting chamber but also a ceremonial hall where the Earl Marischal would receive

The 14th-century keep or tower house

BASEMENT

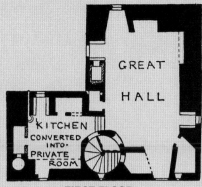

FIRST FLOOR

important guests, a courtroom where he would preside and the common room where daily business was transacted by his officials. It looks bleak now but it used to be a fine room, the walls coated with gleaming plaster and covered in rich hangings, its timber ceiling painted in brilliant colours. The large windows which light it would originally have had hinged wooden shutters in their lower parts, the upper portion being filled with fixed leaded glass panels (similar to the windows in the top floor of Benholm's Lodging). As in some other parts of the castle, the necessary stabilising of the stonework in the 1920s has meant that several of these windows have new dressed stone surrounds.

At the far end, perhaps raised on a dais in front of the fireplace, was the Earl Marischal's table. In the wall to the right of where the table stood is a recess which would have held a sideboard displaying the Keiths' silver tableware. To your left is a doorway cut through the wall to give direct access to the private room in the old kitchen. Next to it is a small latrine built into the thickness of the wall. Behind you is the 'screens passage', a service area where dishes from the kitchen would be laid out ready for serving in the hall. In the corner above the Keep doorway is a small room which could either have been a rather cramped bedroom or else a strongroom for valuables.

The upper floors of the wing held bedrooms, but in the main block above the great hall was the Earl Marischal's private hall and family room, more comfortably furnished than the public great hall below. It had a timber floor which would have been strewn with fresh rushes and when possible with flowers and aromatic herbs. Here he would have discussed private affairs with his advisers, entertained special guests and spent time with his family. In the corner nearest the gatehouse you can see the remains of an elegant 'trefoil' recess set into the wall. This may have been a cupboard for his private possessions or a small shrine where the family could pray in private.

The spiral stairs climb to a 'cap house' which leads on to the parapet running round the tower (see illustration page 2). Sadly this is too dangerous to open to the public. Inside this parapet was a garret with sleeping accommodation suitable for servants and sentries, then on the very top was a look-out platform.

Window of the upper hall with trefoil recess to the left

STOREHOUSE AND STABLES

When the Keep got its extensive new kitchen late in the 16th century, a new Storehouse was built – quite logically right beside the Keep. The Storehouse would have been under the supervision of the Earl Marischal's steward; large supplies had always to be available, less to insure against the threat of a long siege, than to meet the daily needs of the Earl's family and servants.

The larger of the two stores probably held the bulk supplies of grain and tubs of butter and cheeses; the other may have contained salted carcases of cattle and mutton beside barrels of salted fish, salmon, whiting and herring. As a great landholder, the Earl could provide most of these staple supplies from his 'mains' or home farms, or else he would collect them as rents from tenants. Finer exotic foods, like raisins, rice, preserved fruit and spices, which were reserved for the Earl's table, would have been kept in locked cupboards under the careful watch of the steward, who probably lived in one of the apartments above the Storehouse.

Travel was a fact of life for great nobles like the Keiths, who had estates scattered throughout north-east Scotland and were in regular attendance on the King. Hence the extensive Stables where about twelve of the Earl's finest horses – for hunting or cutting a dash at court – would be housed.

The stable block contains many stones salvaged from older buildings; some of the door lintels, for example, are upturned window sills.

Stone from the old chapel re-used in the Stables

In the room nearest the Keep saddles and bridles were probably stored; between this and the actual Stables was a store for the large quantities of horsefeed needed. At the far end of the block are two generous houses for the livery masters, outside one of which is a stone with a Gothic incision, probably re-used from the original chapel. In contrast to their masters, the grooms and stable boys lived in a barrack-like dormitory over the Stables.

SMITHY AND WATERTON'S LODGING

Nearby is the smithy, easily identified by the wonderful big fireplace and chimney. The blacksmith's role was to ensure that the Earl's horses were well shod; but the forge was also a mini industrial unit whose output met most of the needs of the castle's occupants. The smith made or repaired much of the iron work used in the castle, from bolts and hinges for doors, sconces for candles and torches, to gardening tools and pans for the kitchens and brewhouse. His role would become yet more important in times of war; armour would be repaired and weapons sharpened in the forge. During the long siege of 1651-2, it was probably here that the lead shot for the garrison's muskets was cast.

Mary Queen of Scots visited Dunnottar Castle in 1562 and 1564

The Smithy or forge was a mini industrial unit

Across from the Stables is Waterton's Lodging, named after Thomas Forbes, Laird of Waterton, a prominent Covenanter (see pages 26-7) who often stayed with the seventh Earl Marischal. It was built in the late 16th century by the fourth Earl, known as 'William o' the Tower', for his son and daughter-in-law; William lived to a ripe old age and perhaps the limited space in his tower house was testing the patience of all concerned.

'William o' the Tower' was a friend and close adviser to King James V. After the King's death, William fought at the Battle of Pinkie Cleuch, a Scottish defeat by the invading English which led to the five-year-old Mary Queen of Scots being sent off to France for safety. Fifteen years later Mary visited Dunnottar Castle, still in the hands of old William o' the Tower, and this newly built lodging may have housed the young Queen during her visit.

On the ground floor, nearest the Keep, was a large public room, while at the opposite end was a study or private room opening into a rather complicated back entry. Two similar-sized rooms formed the upper floor, and there was accommodation for servants in the attic over the main block and in the picturesque 'cap house' of the stair.

Contemporary images of the castle, such as that on page 2, show a large tower on the Stables side of the cap house. This seems to have been an enormous industrial chimney, built during military occupation in the 17th century.

THE QUADRANGLE WEST RANGE

Now walk to the main buildings at the far end of the rock. With the Chapel on your right and the crumbling hollow square of the Quadrangle in front, it takes a leap of imagination to understand the elegant living brought to the castle through the addition of these purely social and domestic buildings.

Only the greatest amongst the Scottish nobility at the end of the 16th century could afford to remodel their medieval castles in line with the new fashions which were sweeping across England and Renaissance Europe. But the fourth Earl Marischal, old William o' the Tower, was rich, indeed it was said that he could travel from John o' Groats to Berwick, eating and sleeping each night in his own estates. If anyone could rival an English nobleman's seat it was him!

He embarked on construction of the West Range, on your left, in the late sixteenth century. But it was his son George, the fifth Earl Marischal, a distinguished scholar, statesman and founder of Marischal College in Aberdeen, who is primarily responsible for this island of elegance within a medieval fortress. He had spent seven years travelling in Europe, a common way to finish the education of the heirs of the Scottish nobility, and acquired a taste for Continental comfort and splendour.

George, fifth Earl Marischal, close confidant of James VI and builder of the Quadrangle

To the left of the Quadrangle is a square staircase tower, known as the Silver House, which gives access to the enormous long gallery or ballroom, 35 metres long by 4.5 metres wide, running almost the whole length of the first floor. At the far end is a private room which had a balcony giving a superb view out to sea (from the outside you can still see remains of the supports). The gallery itself is described as being 'curiously ceiled with oak and after a very rich form'; to this picture we must add flickering candles in gleaming sconces, silver drinking cups on the window sills, wood-panelled walls covered with heavy tapestries and oil paintings. Imagine a stage with musicians playing on lutes, viols and recorders and through those windows we may just glimpse ladies in shimmering gowns and ruffled knights dancing a stately minuet or pavane!

The Silver House

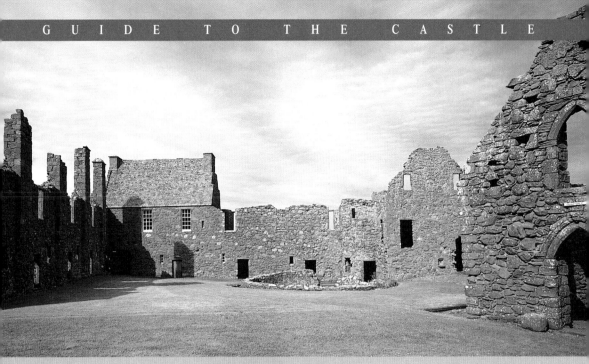

Below the long gallery there are seven 'chambers', probably the quarters of the gentlemen of the Earl Marischal's household. They were built to offer some degree of privacy in contrast to the old arrangement of bedrooms communicating with each other, and provide a rare Scottish example of such a range which occurred commonly in England.

The northern range (straight ahead of you) was the next addition. By adding (with) drawing room, kitchen and dining room, these buildings were changed from a very grand annex into a dwelling. Strangely though, the masterplan must have been changed since we can see that the addition of the north range blocked the door to the furthest of the seven chambers, which then had to be accessed from the bowling green on the far side.

Prominent within the Quadrangle is the well, or more accurately the cistern, since it contains no spring and may at one stage have had water piped to it from the mainland. When excavated last century it was found to be 7.6 metres deep and as for the expected treasure: four brass pans, a small French

sword, five cannon balls, part of a Dutch pot, and one and a half silver teaspoons emerged!

In the other corner, between the West and North Ranges and leading out to the cliffs' is the Water Gate which gave access to a steep path (now very dangerous) leading to a discreet mooring. On the outside corner of the Quadrangle here one can see the 'teeth' that would allow for a wall to stop any seaborne attackers who used this approach from turning right to the bowling green, thus forcing them to enter by the Water Gate which could be easily defended.

With the addition of the North Range, the seventh chamber had to be reached from the bowling green

NORTH AND EAST RANGES

The drawing room seen from the chapel

In the right corner is a porch tower containing the great staircase, a much grander affair than that in the Silver House. Note that the drinking fountain by the door is 20th-century, as is the renovated stair which leads you up into the dining room - spacious and well lit in contrast to the old hall in the Keep. Beyond this room is the renovated drawing room, with a handsome panelled ceiling and a new fireplace lintel in commemoration of George Ogilvy of Barras and others who defended the Honours of Scotland in 1651-2 (See pages 28-31). The floor is laid with a pavement in Arbroath stone, patterned in imitation of that in the Great Hall of Tolquhon Castle, Aberdeenshire.

In the 17th century you could go through from the drawing room either to the long gallery or to the private room with balcony; but we must return through the dining room, at the far end of which is a small retiring or 'speak a word' room.

The room on the right at the top of the main stair is a lobby connecting the Countess' Suite, which forms the upper floor of the East Range of the Quadrangle, and the Marischal's Suite in the range which leads out to the sea. The Countess' Suite, built by George, fifth Earl Marischal, consists of a spacious private chamber, opening into an equally generous bedroom with a smaller closet or dressing room beyond. The Countess' Suite may also, curiously, be reached from some outside steps beside the chapel. It is probably coincidental that the fifth Earl Marischal's Countess deceived him for many years with one Strachan of Thornton, whom she later married; this entrance is not however on record as being called 'Strachan's Stairs'.

As you look at the North Range from the Chapel, the obviously renovated room on the first floor is the (with) drawing room. Beneath it is a range of three cellars. We know that in 1694 these cellars were used (from left to right) as larder, ale cellar and wine cellar.

17th-CENTURY DINING

In the Middle Ages, lords, from kings to humble lairds, ate in the Great Hall with their household. Their status was perhaps stressed by the raising of the lord's table at one end of the hall, lifting him literally above the heads of his dependants, but he ate and drank with them daily. After the meal he might retreat into the privacy of a (with)drawing room, but would often remain in the hall to listen to minstrels and musicians, or to play at cards and gamble on dice with his servants. However since 1603, when James VI of Scotland ascended the English throne, Scotland had been opened to English influences, and her nobility in particular adopted the practices of the English aristocracy. Chief amongst these was what is known as ' keeping state, where a self conscious nobility placed great stress on its status. Now wishing to distance themselves from their social inferiors, lords adopted an 'upstairs downstairs' division of the household, eating and sleeping in private suites while the servants ate in the kitchen or common hall. In place of the trestle tables, benches and straw-strewn floors of the old great halls, the nobility provided themselves with magnificently furnished private chambers where they dined in comfort with their family or social equals. Eating itself became part of the elaborate ritual of keeping state. A lord might sit beneath a canopy of rich cloth, while behind his seat hung a 'cloth of state ', a hanging embroidered with his coat of arms. For all this splendour, the style of food was little changed from earlier ages. Each day the Earl Marischal would be served at least one meat dish, usually beef or mutton, together with fish, chicken or capons, fine white bread, broth, ale, imported claret and on occasion, whisky. Vegetables or fruit were rare additions to the table. And while fine dishes and cutlery had come to replace wooden trenchers and fingers, and meat bones were no longer thrown to the Earl's hunting dogs, hygiene was not much improved: head lice were often seen dropping from the elaborately curled wigs of the nobility to add to the contents of their broth dishes!

The drawing room

MARISCHAL'S SUITE, WHIGS' VAULT AND THE CELLARS

From the lobby at the head of the stair you can enter the Marischal's Suite. This comprises a private room or study and beyond it a bedroom. If you look out of the southern windows of this private room you can just make out, beneath a window in the Countess' Suite, the carved words which appear on the Arms of the Keith Clan: THAY HAIF SAID: QUHAT SAY THAY: LAT YAME SAY, loosely translated as: 'what others say is of no concern to me', a line attributed to the fifth Earl Marischal when criticised for accepting a gift of two abbeys from the king.

THAY HAIF SAID: QUHAT SAY THAY: LAT YAME SAY

The bedroom is known as the King's Chamber, because Charles II slept here in 1650. You can still see the original plaster of the bedroom in some places. Above the fireplace is the reset triangular pediment from

Arms of William, seventh Earl Marischal, and his Countess, Elizabeth Seton

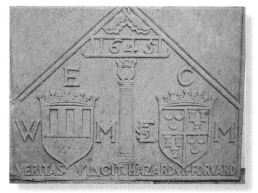

a dormer window with the arms and mottos of the seventh Earl and his wife Elizabeth Seton; it is dated 1645, the year when the Earl abandoned his estates to destruction by Montrose (see pages 26-7).

King Charles II, who slept in the 'King's Chamber' in 1650 and whose insistence that the Episcopalian form of service be used throughout his kingdom led to the appalling treatment of 167 prisoners of conscience in the vault below in 1685

In the wall beside the fireplace is a fine sundial, originally outside but eventually built in here for its preservation. The circular 'loop hole' in the latrine at the far end is interesting as having an internal splay as opposed to the more common and earlier external splay. Experience had taught that the external splay, while excellent for visibility and dispersing smoke, tended to guide bullets to the interior. On a lighter note, the adjacent main window sometimes offers an excellent view of puffins nesting on the cliffs below in spring and early summer (opposite).

Returning to the main stair, we now descend to the vaulted chambers on the ground floor which are linked by a service passage. Turning left at the stairfoot, the furthest doorway leads to the kitchen, a most remarkable example of the chef's domain of those days. Its huge fireplace, spanned by a magnificent arch, 3.8 metres wide, is 3 metres deep; within it on the right-hand side are two dome-vaulted ovens. It is not hard to understand why some chefs in those days died of heatstroke!

In the right-hand wall of the kitchen is a service hatch opening on to the passage through which dishes could be passed and then set on the shelf on the opposite wall ready for carrying up to the dining room. The passage leads through to the back of the east range, where refuse could be carried out and thrown over the cliff.

The left-hand doorway at the end of the passage leads into a vaulted cellar beneath the Marischal's Suite, known as the Whigs' Vault. This is the infamous prison where 167 men and women, whose only crime was refusing to accept the Episcopalian style of church which Charles II had imposed on Scotland, were held for nine weeks with little food and no sanitation. Pause for a minute and imagine being cooped up here with 166 other people for a day, let alone nine weeks!

It appears that a number of the men were actually moved after some days, but to an even smaller and completely airless prison located under the far end of the main vault for which it inevitably provided a drain. You can enter this cellar from the outside. Here the prisoners

The bakery, sometimes frequented by a sad young lady in a green plaid

took it in turns to lie on their bellies and breathe the fresh air that came in through the hole at ground level. Eventually the Governor's wife persuaded her husband to move the women and some of the men to other rooms in the by then semi-derelict castle. Full details of this affair are on pages 32-3.

As you return from the small prison to the passage, you see the doorways to the cellars underneath the Countess' Suite. The first was a storeroom, presumably for malt and barley as the next room was a brewhouse to which a pipe led from the well. At the far end is a bakery with projecting oven by the chapel, and notable for the occasional unnatural presence of a sad young lady in a green plaid.

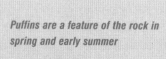

Puffins are a feature of the rock in spring and early summer

THE CHAPEL AND OUTER BUILDINGS

with the exception of two small Gothic windows in the south wall, in the 16th century. The 16th-century Chapel had a belfry above the main door in the west wall and at the opposite end are the remains of what was at one stage a fireplace. Beside this is a small window, obscured when the third side of the Quadrangle was built. There is a nice tale that children who had been too naughty to enter the church listened to the sermon from outside this window as a part of their penance.

On the other side of the wall which connects the Chapel with Waterton's Lodging is the kirkyard or cemetery; only one gravestone is still exposed with the pathetic inscription 'A BARN OF NYN YEARS LYES HERE 1685'. This is almost certainly connected with the imprisonment of the Whigs in that year.

At the south-east corner of the rock is an old sentry box, now the Gents WC, which dominates a small gully, the only approach to the castle not already well protected. To complete our tour, return to the old Keep and take the path to the right of it which leads to a 'pend'; like the two which you passed through on entering.

The south side of the Quadrangle is partly closed off by the oldest surviving building on the rock, the Chapel. The first stone-built Chapel on this site was consecrated in 1276 and burned, with the English garrison within, by William Wallace in 1297 (see page 21). Much of the walling is probably 13th-century, but the Chapel was largely remodelled,

This leads down to 'Wallace's Postern' (back door), the entrance to which is now covered by a low grating, recently adopted as a 'wishing well'. The idea of the Scottish hero leading his men through this narrow entrance to attack the hated English from an

One of the two small Gothic windows

The knife-edge ridge connecting the rock with the mainland

unexpected quarter is an attractive one. However, the evidence is that the 'postern' was built as a secret access to the castle some 400 years after Wallace's death.

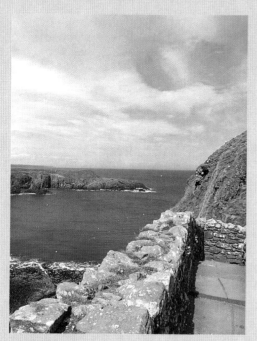

View from the parapet above the barrack room

When the castle was occupied, you could go straight on at this point, to a defensive position on the knife-edge ridge connecting the rock to the mainland, but today this area is extremely unsafe and is closed to the public. A steep stair leads you down past the top floor of Benholm's Lodging where there is a small exhibition. Your way out of the castle is now along the parapet above the old barrack room beside the gatehouse.

But pause to glance over to the 'lion's den' on your right; once, indeed, home to a lion, the favoured pet or mascot of the Earl Marischal. His Countess was not so keen, however, and 'being disturbed by his roaring in the night, caused him to be killed; after which a bear was put in his place, which was so tamed as to present his right or left paw on the Earl holding out his right or left hand'. And so, with this curious sketch of the Earl Marischal's choice of pets – and relationship with his Countess – our tour of this dramatic and evocative Scottish castle draws to a close.

G U I D E

A MISSIONARY STATION

It is 400 years since the birth of Christ. Scotland is divided between four peoples: Scots, Angles, Picts and Britons. The east of the country is held by the Picts; their religion is druidic, their language related to modern Welsh or Breton. We know them primarily from the wonderful sculptured stones which still stand on hillsides and in the villages of the region.

One of the Pictish stones found at Dinnacair

Into this landscape steps Ninian, bringing a new religion, Christianity. Later Scotland's first saint, Ninian worked tirelessly from his base in south-west Scotland to found a chain of churches. One of his chosen sites was Dunnottar.

The attractiveness of Dunnottar as a fortified site is plain to the most unmilitary visitor, but St Ninian also found in this area a peaceful place where his followers would draw spiritual strength. The church would have been a low timber building, made largely of wattle and daub (interlaced wood saplings plastered with mud or clay), with a cluster of thatched cabins around it, housing a more or less permanent community of disciples. From here they spread the Word in north-east Scotland.

No Pictish stones survive on the Dunnottar headland; however, close by, on the isolated rock to the north known as Dinnacair, sculptured stones were found, not just with the familiar Pictish symbols, but also including a fish, traditionally the symbol of Christ. The Celtic Church often had places of retreat on lonely headlands and Dinnacair was very likely such a place for the clergy of the Dunnottar missionary station. If Dunnottar was indeed one of the earliest Christian sites in Pictland, it is logical that the Dinnacair sculptured stones were amongst the very first to include these Christian symbols.

Dunnottar later became a significant Pictish centre and fort. In the late 9th century, when Pictland was becoming Scotland, King Donald II was killed defending Dunnottar against a Viking invasion. He died in vain however, since we learn that the castle was taken and destroyed.

Dunnottar continued to be an important religious site, however. So much so, that when Sir William Keith, the first Earl Marischal, built his tower house here in the 14th century, he was excommunicated by the Bishop of St Andrews for building on a sacred rock. Keith successfully pleaded with the Pope to have the sentence reduced on payment of a suitable fee.

A window which survived William Wallace's burning of the Chapel

BESIEGED BY WILLIAM WALLACE

It is not until 250 years after the Vikings' visit that Dunnottar reappears in history. By this time it has become a castle, not a stone castle as we see it today, but one built from earth and timber.

Dunnottar Castle is one of the exotic locations selected by the cleric who composed the mock epic poem 'Le Roman de Fergus' in the early 13th century, so it was clearly sufficiently well known to have meaning for a contemporary audience of the court circle and Scottish nobility. Later that century, in 1276, a stone parish church in Norman style was consecrated. It was probably built on the site of St Ninian's early chapel; certainly the new building continued to bear the saint's name. Two windows of this chapel survive to this day.

Over the next 100 years Dunnottar was a prized possession in the struggle between the Scots and their dominant English neighbours. The problem arose following the tragic death

William Wallace

of the Scots King Alexander III, closely following those of his three children. King Edward I of England moved quickly to fill the resulting vacuum and when his will was

disputed, he enforced his authority with a heavy hand.

Dunnottar was one of the key castles that Edward occupied as part of his 'overlordship' of Scotland. Resistance to English domination was led by William Wallace, who attacked the castle with an untrained army. Many of the terrified English garrison took refuge in the sanctuary of the chapel, at that time just 21 years old. Wallace burnt chapel, garrison and all. The story is graphically told by 'Blind Harry', a 15th-century poet whose epic poem 'Wallace' (see panel) was an inspiration for the 1996 film 'Braveheart'.

In battle rank, then through the Mearns they march,
And diligently after Southrons search,
Who frightened all before the host do flee,
Unto Dunnottar standing in the sea.
To that great strength they all in haste do throng:
Their numbers then made up four thousand strong.
Some in the church their sanctuary took,
The rest march'd up all to the craigy rock.
With whom the bishop fairly treated so,
To spare their lives if from the land they'd go.
Like fools they on his words would not rely,
Therefore a fire was brought speedily:
Which burnt the church and all those
Southron boys:
Out o'er the rock the rest rush'd with great noise;
Some hung on craigs and loath were to die.
Some lap some fell, some flutter'd in the sea;
And perished all, not one remained alive.

Blind Harry's Wallace.
trans. William Hamilton of Gilbertfield.

IN THE HANDS
OF THE ENGLISH

King Robert the Bruce

smiths 'of the best and most circumspect available', together with a protective force of 100 archers to be 'recruited' from the counties of Norfolk and Suffolk. He authorised that vessels may be commandeered and men impressed from all harbours from the mouth of the Thames northwards 'so far as necessary to the execution of the royal orders, which brook no further delay'. The fortifications would have been largely of wood, but some stones of the castle that we see now were doubtless set in place by these unfortunate English craftsmen plucked roughly from their home soil. We can but hope that their work was approved of by the English King, who visited in July of that year, and that they were eventually allowed home (unlike Sir Thomas Roscelyn, who was killed by the burgesses of Aberdeen, sick of his constant pillaging of their countryside).

Following William Wallace's death, Robert the Bruce took up the struggle. He thought that victory was complete following the Battle of Bannockburn in 1314 where a certain Sir Robert de Keith, the King's Marischal, commanded the cavalry. But 15 years later King Robert was dead and Edward Balliol, a pretender to the Scottish throne, invaded Scotland with English support to claim the throne. Dunnottar was again seized by the English and immediately reinforced.

The urgency with which this was done is remarkable: in March 1336 Edward III of England ordered his favourite Thomas Roscelyn to arrange for carpenters, masons,

Shortly afterwards, the castle was retaken for the Scots by the Regent, Sir Andrew Moray; however, after the custom of the time following a victory, he also thought it best to burn it! By the end of the 14th century, what remained of Dunnottar was in the hands of Sir William Keith, great grandson of Sir Robert de Keith, commander of the cavalry at Bannockburn and the first hereditary Great Marischal of Scotland. It was Sir William who built the earliest parts of the present castle, notably the Keep and the curtain wall. The Keiths continued to play a prominent role as advisers to the monarch and in 1458 Sir William's grandson was made Earl Marischal, the only peer to be styled by his great office of state (see opposite).

A 132294

DUNNOTTAR CASTLE

Proprietor: Per the Factor, Estates Office, Dunecht, Skene, Aberdeenshire.
www.dunnottarcastle.co.uk

ADMISSION BY TICKET ONLY
£6.00 (VAT Inclusive)

The attention of visitors is drawn to the terms and conditions of entry, and visitors should note that these are included in the contract of entry. The terms and conditions of entry include a specific provision that the Proprietor will not be liable for any damage or loss to property or animal(s) of any person who enters the Castle and relative grounds.

A 132293

DUNNOTTAR CASTLE

Proprietor: Per the Factor, Estates Office, Dunecht, Skene, Aberdeenshire.
www.dunnottarcastle.co.uk

ADMISSION BY TICKET ONLY
£6.00 (VAT Inclusive)

The attention of visitors is drawn to the terms and conditions of entry, and visitors should note that these are included in the contract of entry. The terms and conditions of entry include a specific provision that the Proprietor will not be liable for any damage or loss to property or animal(s) of any person who enters the Castle and relative grounds.

A 132292

DUNNOTTAR CASTLE

Proprietor: Per the Factor, Estates Office, Dunecht, Skene, Aberdeenshire.
www.dunnottarcastle.co.uk

ADMISSION BY TICKET ONLY
£6.00 (VAT Inclusive)

The attention of visitors is drawn to the terms and conditions of entry, and visitors should note that these are included in the contract of entry. The terms and conditions of entry include a specific provision that the Proprietor will not be liable for any damage or loss to property or animal(s) of any person who enters the Castle and relative grounds.

Sir Robert de Keith commanded the cavalry at the Battle of Bannockburn

THE MARSHAL OR MARISCHAL

The rise of the Keiths, Marischals of Scotland, was completed in 1458 when King James II created them Earls Marischal, but the origins of their office were much humbler. Marshals were part of the domestic establishments of kings and great noblemen, having the responsibility of overseeing the supply and care of their masters' horses. At first they were relatively unimportant, but from the 12th century there is a specific office of 'king's marischal' and a rise in its status, with subsequent holders usually being of knightly rank.

The king's marischal was subordinate to the king's constable, who was responsible for military organisation and for the security and peace of the royal court. The marischal probably held military responsibilities, as would be expected of a knight, but one of his principal duties was as holder of a court for settling disputes between the king's servants. One 14th-century account of the king's household describes the constable and marischal as having a sphere of jurisdiction, extending to 12 leagues (about 36 miles) around the court.

By this time, along with the constable and the steward, the marischal had become one of the three great officers of the king's household, and was usually a man of baronial (as opposed to knightly) rank. During the Wars of Independence the military role predominated and the marischalcy was entrusted by Robert the Bruce to Sir Robert de Keith who commanded the cavalry at the Battle of Bannockburn. Later the king confirmed the position of Great Marischal as the heritable possession of Sir Robert and his male heirs.

The Keith Marischals featured prominently as military captains in the service of both Robert I and his son, but later their wartime role diminished and the title had become largely honorific. The marischal and his kin rose to be one of the leading families of baronial rank in the north east of Scotland, and it was this landed power rather than possession of the marischalcy which gave them their dominant political role. When Sir William Keith was elevated to an earldom, the transition from a functional to a ceremonial role was complete.

A list of the Keiths of Dunnottar, Marischals of Scotland, is given on page 36.

E N T E R T A I N I N G   R O Y A L T Y

Every Scottish castle worthy of the name has been visited by Mary Queen of Scots and Dunnottar qualified in November 1562. The 19 year-old Queen was perhaps still in a state of shock having witnessed, two days before, the botched execution of one of her admirers, John Gordon. Young Gordon's father, the Marquis of Huntly, had led an unsuccessful rebellion against the Queen, culminating in defeat at the Battle of Corrichie near Aberdeen.

Standard of the Earl Marischal of Scotland, carried at the Battle of Flodden Field, 1513

Staying with the Earls Marischal for a few days was by no means unusual for the monarch. We know for certain that Mary's grandfather, King James IV, was entertained here on 15 October 1503. Indeed 18 shillings were given to a child who pleased the king by playing on the monocordis. Ten years later the king was killed at the Battle of Flodden Field, along with the two sons of the Earl Marischal,

an event which led to young William becoming the fourth Earl aged just 29.

Mary returned to Dunnottar in September 1564 and her son, James VI, particularly enjoyed the seat of the Earls Marischal. He spent ten days here in June 1580, primarily hunting but also, curiously, presiding over a meeting of the Privy Council. His host was the fourth Earl, now known as 'William o' the Tower' because towards the end of his life he seldom left his tower house. William had been an adviser to the king's mother (tragically still in prison in England) and to his grandfather James V. Now aged 80 and in the last year of his life, the role of host to the 14 year-old monarch and his retinue must have been a little taxing!

Mary was executed by her cousin Queen Elizabeth of England in 1587. However, it seems that her son shed few tears and the sport-loving King of Scotland continued to enjoy his holidays at Dunnottar. He clearly had strong ties with William's grandson, George the fifth Earl Marischal: he continued to correspond with his friend even after taking up residence in London, after his accession to the English throne in 1603.

A footnote to this period is that in 1595 a certain John Crichton, condemned to death in an orgy of witch hunting at Aberdeen, was taken to Dunnottar Castle to be burnt at the stake. We know that Dunnottar was sometimes used as a prison, but history does not relate whether it was also the approved burning site for all local witches, or whether this was some kind of particular circumstance or last request.

JAMES IV = MARGARET TUDOR
(1472-1513)   (daughter of Henry VII of England)

JAMES V = MARY OF GUISE
(1512-1542)

MARY QUEEN OF SCOTS = HENRY
(1542-1587)   STEWART
                                           LORD DARNLEY

JAMES VI OF SCOTLAND
(JAMES I OF ENGLAND)
(1566-1625)

King James VI of Scotland, who called a meeting of the Privy Council at Dunnottar Castle during a hunting trip

T H E   P R I V Y   C O U N C I L

Medieval Scottish kings took advice from a small and informal group of councillors who could gather quickly to discuss urgent business. This body, known as the 'secret' or 'privy' council due to the oaths of silence concerning its business sworn by the members, grew into the chief instrument of government. Membership of the council was decided by the king. Naturally, leading noblemen were included, partly in recognition of their regional dominance, partly as a sop to a class who guarded jealously their traditional role as royal counsellors. Mostly, however, its members were those in regular attendance on the king, in effect the chief functionaries and office holders of the royal household including the Earl Marischal. The Privy Council was far more important than parliament in the daily life of the kingdom. The sheer volume of business meant that the council, which met in Edinburgh, was in almost permanent session. It was very unusual for it to meet at a place such as Dunnottar (when only seven members were present). Membership ranged in numbers between 35 and 50, but records show that the actual average attendance was eight to ten.

By the early 17th century when James VI moved to England, its most active members were judges and career civil servants, men whose professionalism and competence smoothed the running of government in the absence of the king. Some councillors still enjoyed access to the king's ear, but mostly it was the executive for decisions made elsewhere. Increasingly, James sent instructions which he expected to be enforced without question; the element of consultation was disappearing. From 1660 to 1688, the Council's principal role was to impose Charles II's will in Scotland, especially in matters of religious policy. After the Act of Union in 1703, a separate Scottish Privy Council was redundant and in 1708 it was formally abolished.

M O N T R O S E   A N D
T H E   M A R I S C H A L

James Graham, First Marquis of Montrose

William Keith, seventh Earl Marischal

The turbulent events of the mid-17th century in Scotland are dominated by the dashing figure of James Graham, Marquis of Montrose, who led those Scots who signed the National Covenant for Religious Freedom (and against royal religious diktat). Initially he led the Covenanting Army but later, when Oliver Cromwell clearly threatened the very existence of the monarchy, he dramatically switched sides to command the King's army in Scotland.

Those who had signed the National Covenant or supported it were called Covenanters; the seventh Earl Marischal was a Covenanter and joined Montrose's Covenanting Army in 1639 not just with men, but also in an early skirmish against the Government forces at nearby Megray Mill, with 'several feeld peeces' and 'two brasse battering pieces, half canone'.

Montrose was not counting on an easy victory and had commanded that the Dunnottar Castle gates should be left open, just in case the battle went against them. It did not however, and Montrose and the Marischal then advanced on Aberdeen which was duly taken for the Covenanters.

When Montrose next met the Marischal, 6 years later, it was not as an ally but as a heavy-handed foe since the Civil War had now begun. The years had apparently drained the warlike spirit of the Earl Marischal, who abandoned his tenants and property to the Royalist Army, shutting himself up in Dunnottar with a few supporters and a select band of 16 ministers of religion, including the notorious Presbyterian firebrand Andrew Cant. Montrose tried to win over his old companion in arms but, probably at Cant's instigation, the Earl declined the Royalist Captain's offer to negotiate. Several times Montrose sent his envoy to the gate but received no answer, at which, the chronicler

Charles I Scottish copper 'turner', found at Dunnottar

tells us, he was 'heichlie offendit'. So much so that he set fire to every house, barn, stable and even ship in the baronies of Dunnottar, Fetteresso and Cowie; even Stonehaven beyond was burnt to the ground (see panel).

The next time Montrose came to these parts it was as a fugitive to board a boat from Stonehaven to Norway and exile, following the defeat of the Royalist armies and the execution of King Charles I. So swings the pendulum of war.

MONTROSE'S BURNING OF STONEHAVEN

Whereupon Montrose, on 21st March, began and burnt up the barnyards of Dunnottar, houses, grain and all which the Earl, his lady and the rest within the place saw; then (he) fired the tollbooth of Stonehaven, wherein there were stores of barley and oats, and the whole town also, being the king's royal burgh, with all of the cornyards, houses and buildings, except the said James Clerk's building wherein Montrose himself was quartered. They plundered a ship lying in the harbour then set it on fire along with the fishing boats lying there. They burnt up the whole town of Cowie, houses, buildings, grain and cornyards and suchlike; (they) plundered all the goods, horses, cattle, sheep, which they could get. They plundered the persons of Dunnottar house, then set the same on fire. It is said the people of Stonehaven and Cowie came out man and woman, children at their feet and children in their arms, crying, howling and weeping, praying the Earl for God's cause to save them from this fire as soon as it was kindled. But the poor people got no answer, nor knew they where to go with their children. Lamentable to see!

John Spalding, "Memorials of the Trubles in Scotland and in England," ed. J Stuart

SAVING THE HONOURS OF SCOTLAND

**George Ogilvy of Barras,
Governor of Dunnottar Castle 1651-2**

Oliver Cromwell, self-proclaimed Lord Protector

In July 1650, the young King Charles II arrived in north-east Scotland and was heading south to give battle for his father's kingdom. On the way he stayed at Dunnottar. But only two months earlier, Montrose, the King's Viceroy, having recently returned to Scotland had been hung drawn and quartered in Edinburgh by friends of the Earl Marischal as punishment for his support of the King. One may imagine that conversation over their dinner of 'fresh local salmon' was perhaps a little stilted.

In England, Oliver Cromwell, the self-proclaimed Lord Protector, was enraged at the young King's arrival and invaded Scotland. In some haste Charles II was crowned at Scone, but the crown and the other coronation regalia, together comprising the 'Honours of Scotland' could not be returned to Edinburgh Castle, which had now been taken by Cromwell's 'Roundhead' Army. Cromwell had already destroyed the English crown jewels and the Honours of Scotland, the most potent remaining icon of the monarchy, were next on his list. His army was fast advancing on Scone and the King ordered 'the Erle of Marchell to cause transport the saidis Honouris to the hous of Dunnottor, thair to be kept by him till farther ordouris'.

And it was not an easy task to transport the Honours across Scotland, now largely controlled by Cromwell. A sword 1.3 metres long with handle 43 cms wide, together with crown and sceptre, are not easily concealed and the story goes that a certain Mrs Drummond, wife of the minister of Moneydie, a village near Scone, took on the task. Disguised as a peasant woman, and with nothing but her native wit and courage to protect her, she rode to Dunnottar, visiting various market towns on her way, carrying some bulky sacks of wool within which the Honours of Scotland were concealed. We also know that King Charles' private papers and 'all the King's rich hangins and bedds, plate and other furniture' were held for security at the castle.

Unfortunately, very soon afterwards the Earl Marischal, along with several other Scottish noblemen, was surprised by a troop of Cromwell's horse and he became Cromwell's prisoner in the Tower of London. George Ogilvy of Barras, a friend of the Earl Marischal and an accomplished soldier, was appointed Governor of the castle, (presumably by letter from the Tower) and he assembled a garrison of 69 men and 42 guns, many less than he thought necessary for the task.

Steadily Cromwell's armies tightened their hold on Scotland. Early in September 1651, Roundhead troops appeared before the castle and camped on the Black Hill between it and Stonehaven. Very few details of the siege operations are known, but the position of the castle meant that any attempt to take it by storm was futile and the buildings on the rock had nothing to fear from anything, save the heaviest cannon - which was not at first available.

Throughout the winter the small garrison held out, relying on dangerous sorties by boat and under cover of darkness to seize or bargain for supplies. In May 1652, the only place in Scotland that still flew the royal flag was Dunnottar Castle, but the English now got their siege artillery into position and the formal bombardment began. Twelve shells were thrown into the 'great tower' resulting in the deaths of seven men, and further reducing the garrison to 'a mere handful (we are told) in comparison of the number then requisite to defend the place.... and all of 'em day and

night upon duty [and] extremely fatigu'd yet they maintain'd their respective posts valorously'. For ten days they were 'exposed to the havock of bombs and the shoaks of thundering cannon'.

Despite his protestations, Ogilvy clearly had a certain amount of firepower to hold out against Cromwell since it is later reported that Cromwell's forces carried off on surrender 'twenty one brass cannon, one hundred and forty fixed muskets and many firelocks, twenty six barrels of powder and ten chests of musket

The Honours of Scotland

balls'. But the King, writing from Paris, could offer him no guidance and there was no realistic prospect of any Royalist forces coming to his aid. Meanwhile the castle and its garrison were being systematically destroyed. Discretion was clearly the better part of valour here and on 24 May 1652, after an impressive resistance of eight months, Ogilvy of Barras surrendered 'with all the honours of war'.

The besieging forces now looked forward to laying hands on the Honours of Scotland and taking them with pride to their London masters. The disappointment was cruel.

IN COMMEMORATION OF THE DEFENCE OF THE HONOURS OF SCOTLAND
FROM SEPTEMBER 1651 TO MAY 1652
BY GEORGE OGILVY OF BARRAS GOVERNOR OF DUNNOTTAR
AND THE HELP GIVEN BY HIS WIFE ELIZABETH DOUGLAS
AND BY HER KINSWOMAN ANNE LINDSAY

The fireplace lintel in the drawing room in commemoration of the defence of the Honours of Scotland by George Ogilvy of Barras, his wife Elizabeth Douglas and her kinswoman Anne Lindsay

The King's private papers, carefully stitched into a flat belt round her middle, had been smuggled through the besieging lines by Anne Lindsay, a relative of Ogilvy's wife. As to the Honours, there are several versions of the story, but all agree that the main credit belongs to Mrs Grainger, wife of the minister of the kirk at Kinneff, a village several miles south. She herself may have secreted crown and sceptre under her skirts during an approved compassionate visit to the castle and ridden out under the noses of the enemy.

A more likely story is that crown, sceptre and sword were lowered over the side of the castle and received by one of Mrs Grainger's serving women, there on pretence of gathering seaweed. Stored within a humble creel and covered in weed, the Honours of Scotland were unceremoniously carried from the field of battle. They were hidden first, it is said, at the bottom of the bed in the manse until the minister could bury them more securely in the kirk!

After eight months the besieging troops were therefore rewarded with a few sticks of the King's furniture. Quite understandably they were not content with this and sadly the castle had to pay the penalty. We read that the chapel was demolished and the room at the end of the Countess' Suite 'suffered prejudices', but this is a small part of the substantial damage inflicted by the victors. Ogilvy of Barras and his lady were imprisoned in the castle but neither would give up the secret; Ogilvy survived to tell the tale but his wife died from the effects of her treatment.

The Honours remained in the custody of Mr Grainger at Kinneff until the restoration of the monarchy in 1660; every now and then the

The crown, sceptre and sword had been lowered over the side of the castle rock and received by a serving woman, there on the pretence of gathering seaweed

Burial of the Honours of Scotland in Kinneff Kirk

minister and his wife would go to the kirk at the dead of night to lift them from their hiding places underneath the paving stones to ensure all was well. At the opening of the Scottish Parliament the following year, the Earl Marischal carried the crown, his brother George (later the eighth Earl) the sceptre, and his younger brother John (later the first Earl of Kintore) the sword.

The seventh Earl thus upheld the traditions of the Marischalcy but his finances had suffered severely, partly through his own profligacy, but mainly due to the continuous troubles. He spent most of the rest of his life in London where he could more easily hide his poverty. The Honours meanwhile have their own story, which can be heard at Edinburgh Castle where they are on permanent display.

Kinneff Kirk and the memorial to the Reverand James Grainger which is inside it

THE WHIGS' VAULT

Dunnottar Castle was destined never to recover from the damage caused by Cromwell's siege guns and by those who supplanted Ogilvy in its command. The Keep was now open to the elements and the 'stately halls' had been rifled of their contents. The Earl Marischal had not the means to make good the damage and for the next 40 years Dunnottar was a military depot.

The Whigs' Vault

Despite the support that he had enjoyed from his Scottish subjects and the vows he had made at his Scottish coronation nine years earlier, Charles II vigorously promoted Episcopacy, a Church structure based on bishops, and outlawed Presbyterianism, the religion of the Covenanters, of most Scots, and indeed of the Earls Marischal. Covenanters now had to worship in secret, risking attack by the military. The inevitable revolt came first from the Presbyterians of south-west Scotland, where they were known as Whiggamores (from the Scots word for whey, and giving rise to the political term Whig).

And so we come to the darkest chapter in the history of Dunnottar. The fury of the authorities reached fever pitch when the Duke of Monmouth, the King's illegitimate son, endeavoured to take the British throne by force. In Scotland the ill-fated rebellion was led by the Duke of Argyll. It was then that a body of Covenanting prisoners, 122 men and 45 women, who refused to acknowledge the new prayer book in particular and the King's supremacy in spiritual matters in general, were transported 'for security' to Dunnottar Castle. The whole band was herded indiscriminately into the gloomy cellar since known as the 'Whigs' Vault' and they remained in the castle with little food and no sanitation from 24 May 1685 to the end of July.

The panel gives an extract from the 'The History of the Sufferings of the Church of Scotland'. This account is certainly overstated in some respects – it is obvious, for example, that the vault has more than one window, but it is the only account we have and it certainly offers us a graphic version of events.

We know for sure that 37 Whigs finally agreed to take the oath of allegiance and were released; 25 escaped, of which 15 were recaptured and two fell to their deaths from

HERE LYES IOHN STOT IAMES ATCHI
SON IAMES RUSSELL & WILLIAM BRO
UN AND ONE WHOSE NAME WEE HAVE
NOT GOTTEN AND TWO WOMEN WHOSE
NAME SALSO WEE KNOW NOT AND TWO
WHO PERISHED COMEING DOUNE THE ROCK
ONE WHOSE NAME WAS IAMES WATSON
THE OTHER NOT KNOWN WHO ALL DIED
PRISONER SIN DUNNOTTAR CASTLE
ANNO 1685 FOR THEIR ADHERENCE
TO THE WORD OF GOD AND SCOTLANDS
COVENANTED WORK OF REFORMA
TION·   REV· 11 CH· 12 VERSE

Wording on the Covenanters' Stone, Dunnottar Kirkyard

the rock in the attempt. A memorial to these two and a further five who died, 'The Covenanters' Stone', is in Dunnottar Kirkyard. The rest were deported to the West Indies but we are told that about 70 of the remainder died of fever on the journey or shortly afterwards.

TREATMENT OF THE PRISONERS

At Dunnottar, they were received by George Keith of White ridge, Sheriff Depute of the Mearns. This large company was thrust into a dark vault underground... It was full of mire, ankle deep and had but one window towards the sea. So throng were they in it that they could not sit without leaning one upon another...They had no access to ease nature and many of them were faint and sickly...The prisoners had nothing allowed them but what was paid for, and money was paid for cold water. And when the soldiers had brought in barrels of water and had sold it out in parcels to them until they began to weary of it, they would pour it into the vault to incommode them the more. Considerable numbers of them died and no wonder, through such hardships; and it was boasted of as an undeserved favour by the soldiers, that they received the dead corpses and disposed of them as they pleased.

It was no great wonder that under such grievous hardships they essayed all innocent methods for their own safety. In order to do this they endeavoured and got at length out by the window in the vault which was just over the sea, one night, and crept along a most dangerous rock , to the utmost hazard of their lives; and indeed it was one to ten that they were not either crushed by the fall or drowned in the sea. Some twenty five of them escaped before the alarm was given ...

Fifteen of them were apprehended and it was a wonder that all of them were not catched , being so weak that they were not able to flee far...Such as were seized were most barbarously used...when brought back to the prison they were put in the guard house, bound and laid on their backs upon a form and their hands bound to the foot of the form, and a fiery match put betwixt every finger of both hands. This was continued for three hours without intermission.

Extract from 'The Sufferings of the Kirk of Scotland'

THE JACOBITE REBELLIONS AND THE LAST EARL MARISCHAL

George, the eighth Earl Marischal, was amongst the first to proffer allegiance to the Protestant William of Orange who seized the throne in 1688 from the Roman Catholic James VII of Scotland and II of England. Whigs and Covenanters were once more in the ascendancy and later that year we know that the Earl Marischal was appointed Captain of a 60 man garrison at Dunnottar by the new sovereigns, William III and Mary.

In 1695 the ninth Earl Marischal managed to regain possession of Dunnottar, but after 44 years of Army occupation this was a symbolic victory and restored to the Earls Marischal merely a barracks, not anything resembling a family home.

Over the past 60 years of civil strife, the Earls Marischal had contrived so to juggle their allegiance to the normally conflicting causes of King and Covenant that, despite a very high profile in the kingdom, they had literally kept their heads albeit their fortune was sadly depleted.

However, the ninth Earl seemed to lack the judgement of his forebears; unlike his father he openly opposed King William and supported the Roman Catholic James VII and II, now in exile. Supporters of the exiled Stewarts were known as 'Jacobites' (from Jacobus, the latin for James). James II's son, known as 'The Old Pretender', made an attempt to take the crown by force with French assistance in 1707. It was a slightly farcical operation – no invader even set foot

The Old Pretender lands at Peterhead, December 1715. He went on to spend Christmas with the Earl Marischal at one of his houses near Dunnottar.

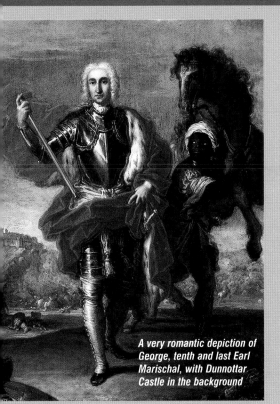

A very romantic depiction of George, tenth and last Earl Marischal, with Dunnottar Castle in the background

and both Pretender and Earl Marischal escaped to France.

King George I was not inclined to exhibit goodwill and in 1716 the tenth Earl Marischal was convicted of treason and incurred the forfeiture of his estates. After a distinguished career abroad, he returned to Scotland in 1763, having been pardoned at the request of Frederick the Great of Prussia. Sadly he did not marry and with him the title died out.

Meanwhile the castle had been sold to the York Building Company, which stripped from it everything of value, leaving only a shell. The Keith family did re-acquire their estates in 1727 and the castle remained in their hands until 1873 but the buildings were not maintained. And so, until 1925 when Lady Cowdray (advised by the distinguished Aberdeen architect Dr William Kelly) embarked on a programme of urgently needed repair, the castle was for over 200 years no more than a romantic relic and a source of building material.

on land - but the Earl Marischal was identified as a leader and imprisoned; he was released later in a gesture of goodwill and took his seat in the House of Lords at Westminster.

The tenth Earl was an officer in the British Army, but on the accession of George I, he was relieved of his commission since the Duke of Argyll had suggested that he was 'suspect' that is, a Jacobite sympathiser. Whether or not this was true, thus rebuffed he was perhaps understandably quick to espouse the Jacobite cause the following year, 1715, when Scottish supporters of the Old Pretender raised the Jacobite flag once again.

The young Earl Marischal commanded a squadron at the Battle of Sherrifmuir and amongst the cannon that supported the Jacobite army were some from Dunnottar Castle. The Pretender arrived at Peterhead on 22 December and spent Christmas at the Earl Marischal's house of Fetteresso near Dunnottar but the rising was already doomed

The Earl Marischal of Scotland's Arms, illustrated about 1715

THE KEITHS OF DUNNOTTAR CASTLE

Sir Robert Keith (d. 1332) Cavalry commander at Bannockburn; created Great Marischal by King Robert the Bruce

grandson: Sir Robert Keith (d.1346) Accompanied King David II to France

brother: Sir Edward Keith

son: Sir William Keith (d.1410) Built the Keep at Dunnottar

son: Sir Robert Keith (d.1430) Acted as hostage in England for James I

son: Sir William Keith (d. 1463) Created Earl Marischal by James II

son: William, 2nd Earl (d.1483)

son: William, 3rd Earl (d.1530) Supported James III against barons; both sons killed at Battle of Flodden Field

grandson: William, 4th Earl (1501-1581) 'William o' the Tower'; the richest earl in Scotland

grandson: George, 5th Earl (1553-1623) Arranged James VI's marriage to Anne of Denmark; founded Marischal College in Aberdeen.

son: William, 6th Earl (d.1635) Officiated at coronation of Charles I; spent most of the family fortune

son: William, 7th Earl (d.1661) Covenanter, tangled with Montrose; imprisoned during Civil War

brother: George, 8th Earl (d.1694) Colonel George Keith of Aden

son: William, 9th Earl (d.1712) Jacobite sympathiser; sat as a peer in Parliament at Westminster

son: George, 10th and last Earl (1692-1778) Leading role in Jacobite rising of 1715; life in exile, died in Prussia